# Pulleys

written by Caroline Rush
and
illustrated by Mike Gordon

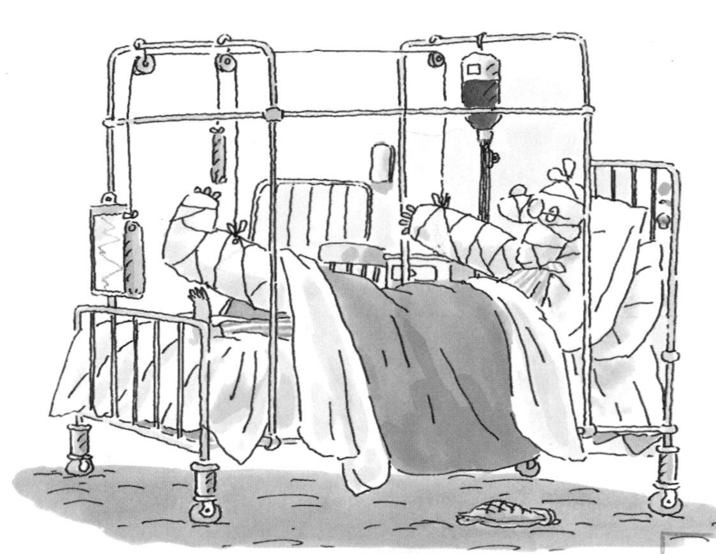

an imprint of Hodder Children's Books

# Simple Science

Wheels and Cogs
Slopes
Levers
Pulleys

**Series Editor**: Catherine Baxter
**Book Editors**: Sue Barraclough and Sarah Doughty

First published in Great Britain in 1996
by Wayland (Publishers) Ltd
This edition printed in 2001 by Hodder Wayland,
an imprint of Hodder Childen's Books



**British Library Cataloguing in Publication Data**
Rush, Caroline
Pulleys. – (Simple science)
1. Pulleys – Juvenile literature 2. Power transmission
Juvenile literature
I. Title II. Gordon, Mike, 1948 –
621.8'5

ISBN 0 7502 3405 9

Typeset by MacGuru
Printed and bound in Hong Kong

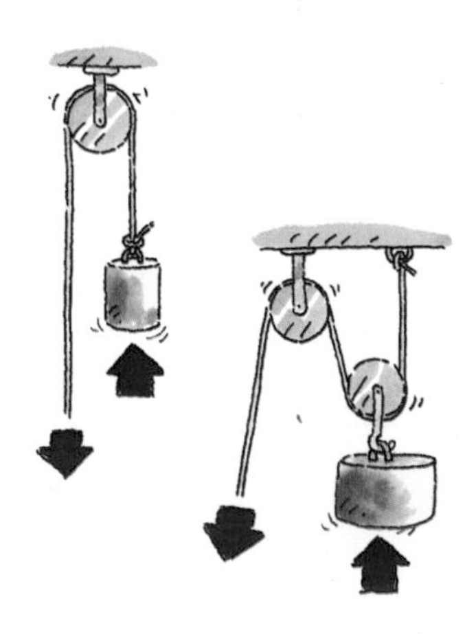

# Contents

Our world would be a very different place without machines to help us.

A pulley is a simple lifting machine.

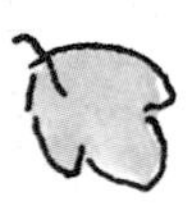

The idea for a pulley may have begun when someone threw a rope over a tree branch to help them to lift a heavy load.

They discovered that it was easier to lift a heavy weight by pulling downwards.

You attach one end of the rope to the object you want to lift and pass the rope around the groove of the wheel. When you pull the other end of the rope, you can raise the object.

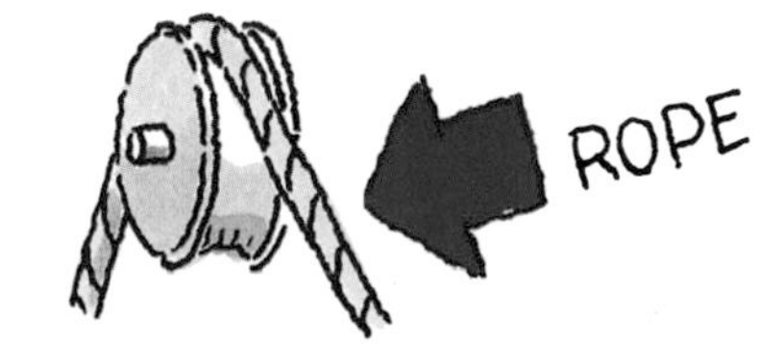


Today's pulleys are made up of a wheel with a groove around the rim and a rope.

Sometimes pulleys are made to raise something high.

It is much easier to use a pulley than to climb up a flagpole and put the flag on top.

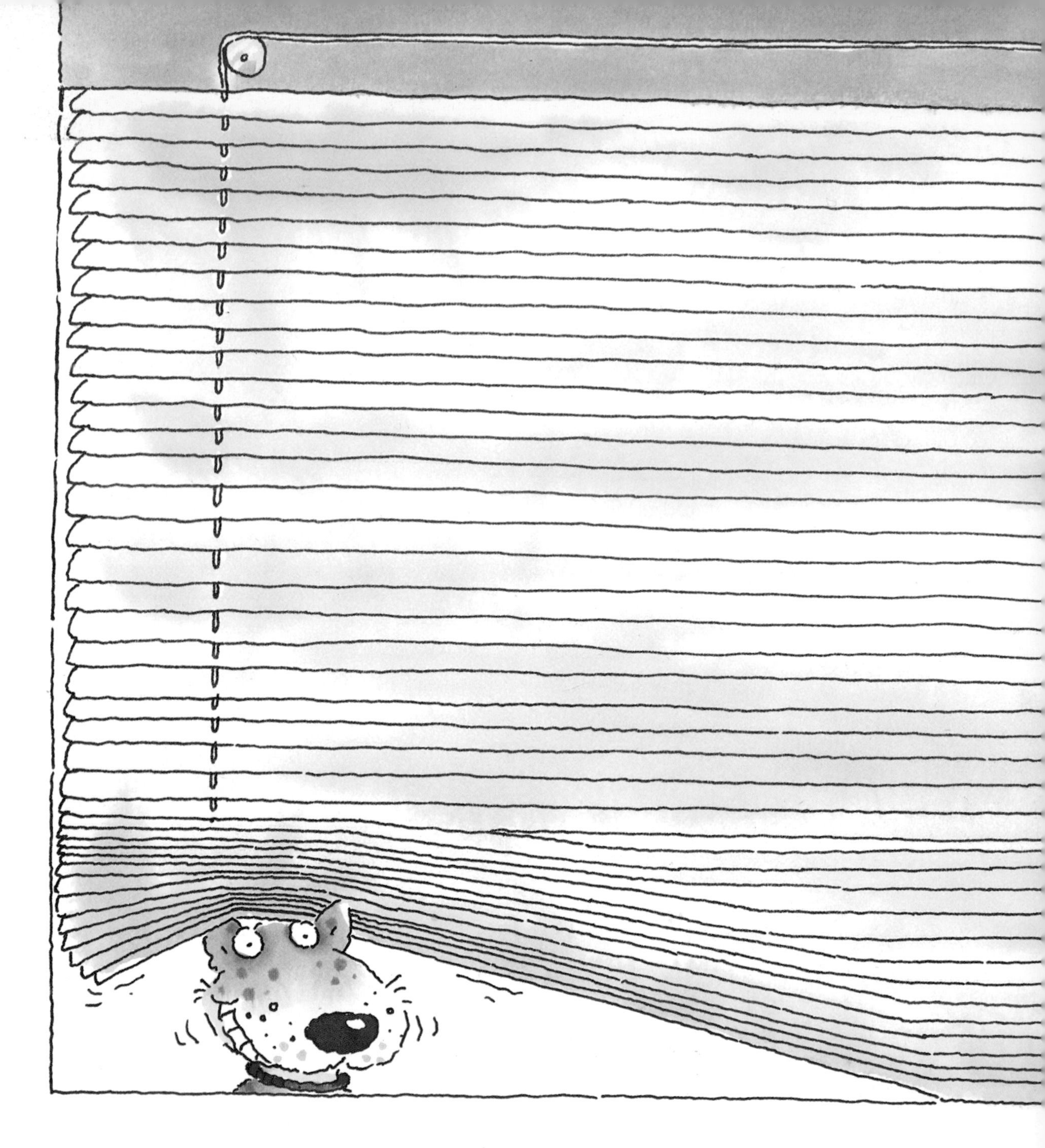

You use a pulley to raise a blind.

You may even be attached to a pulley in hospital.

Pulleys are also used to lift heavy loads. It is easier to pull downwards to lift a heavy weight because you can use your own body weight. Your body acts as a counter-weight.

The more pulley wheels you use, the easier the job of lifting becomes. Using two pulley wheels you can lift something twice as heavy as you can with one pulley wheel.

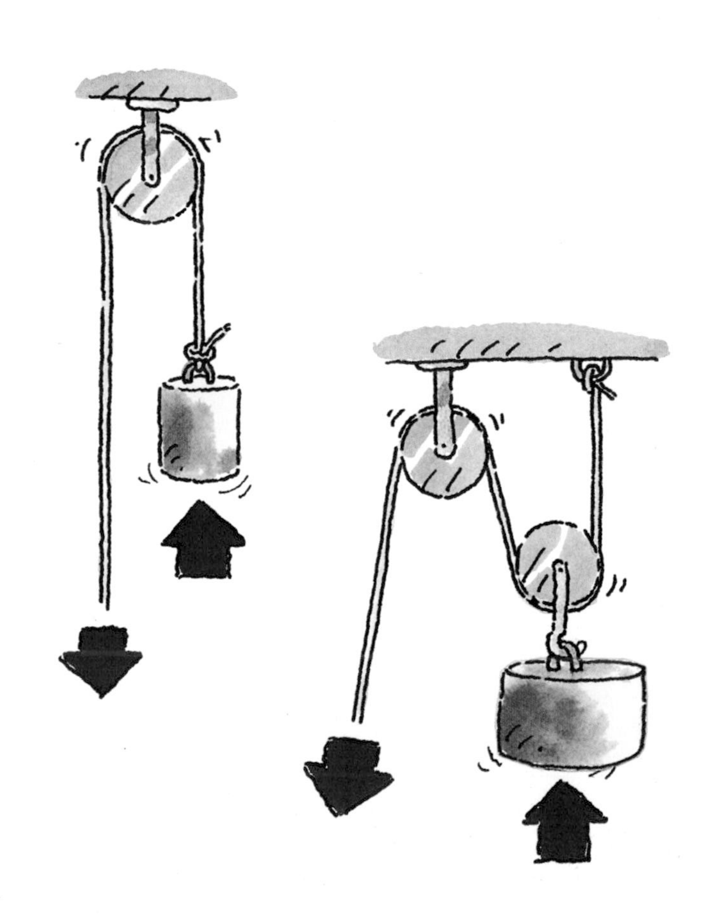

Experiment 1
Experiment 2

Three pulley wheels let you lift something three times as heavy.

Cranes use lots of pulley wheels all together so they can lift really heavy loads from place to place.

When you travel in a lift, you are using a pulley. The lift car is raised by strong cables around a pulley wheel.

An electric motor drives the pulley to raise the lift.

MOTOR
PULLEY
CABLE
LIFT
COUNTER
WEIGHT

## Make your own pulley flagpole

You will need:
2 plastic bottle tops
2 one inch nails
30 cm length of square wooden dowling
Cereal box
PVA glue
String
An adult to help you

1. Ask an adult to nail one bottle top to the top of the wooden dowling and one about 20 cm farther down. They must be loose enough to turn.

2. Turn the cereal box on its side and mark around the base of the dowling. Cut out the hole and slot your flag pole in its base. Decorate the base.

3. Cut out a paper flag and colour it with your own design. Fold over one edge.

4. Lay your string along the fold with the centre in the middle of the flag. Glue the edge down. Leave to dry.

5. Tie the string around the bottle tops so that it is quite taught. Now when you pull down on one side of the string, you will hoist your flag!

# Glossary

| | |
|---|---|
| **Cable** | A very strong rope, often made of metal. |
| **Counter-weight** | A weight used to pull down the end of a rope when an object is being lifted at the other end. |
| **Crane** | A large machine used for lifting very heavy objects. |
| **Load** | The weight of an object that is moved by a machine. |
| **Pulley** | A wheel with a rope around it used to lift an object up. |
| **Rim** | The outer edge of a wheel. |

# Notes for adults

Simple Technology is a series of elementary books designed to introduce young children to the everyday machines that make our lives easier, and the basic principles behind them.

For millions of years people have been inventing and using machines to make work easier. These machines have been constantly modified and redesigned over the years to make them more sophisticated and more successful at their task. This is really what technology is all about. It is the process of applying knowledge to make work easier.

In these books, children are encouraged to explore the early inspirations for machines, and the process of modification that has brought them forward in their current state, and in doing so, come to an understanding of the design process.

The simple text and humorous illustrations give a clear explanation of how these machines actually work, and experiments and activities give suggestions for further practical exploration.

## Suggestions for further activities

- Visit a building site and look at how pulleys are used there, i.e. to lift building materials up scaffolding, within cranes, etc.

- Experiment using different weights with a real pulley wheel. Can you add extra pulley wheels to enable you to lift heavier weights.

- Make a display of pictures from magazines or catalogues of different machines or pulleys to help them to lift things up.

# Books to read

**Machines at Work** by Alan Ward (Watts, 1993)
**How things Work** by Brian Knapp (Atlantic Europe Publishing, 1991)
**The Way it Works/Motion** by Philip Sauvain (Heinemann, 1991)
**Starting Technology/Machines** by John Williams (Wayland, 1991)
**Experiment with Movement** by Brian Murphy (Watts, 1991)
**Simple Science/Push and Pull** by Mike and Maria Gordon (Wayland, 1995)

## Adult reference

**The Way things Work** by David Macaulay (Dorling Kindersley, 1988)
Available as CD Rom (Dorling Kindersley, 1994)

# Index